Derek

'And it shall be like a little stream,
And the little stream shall become a river,
And the river shall become a great river,
The great river shall become a sea,
And the sea shall become a mighty ocean.'

THE MAN BEHIND THE MINISTRY

The Study Guide

Derek Prince THE MAN BEHIND THE MINISTRY – The Study Guide

Published by Derek Prince Ministries–UK

ISBN 1-901144-18-3

This Study Guide compiled by Linda Finley-Day, Summit Publishing Ltd.

Printed in the United Kingdom by Creative Print and Design (Wales), Ebbw Vale

1 2 3 4 5 6 7 8 9 10 / 07 06 05 04

Contents

SUGGESTIONS ON HOW TO USE THE STUDY GUIDE

Derek's life has been an inspiration to what must be millions of people all over the globe, which is why *Derek Prince – the Man Behind the Ministry* can be such a valuable tool in the right hands. The example of Derek's life continues to teach and draw us to the living Word of God. To this end, we have produced *The Study Guide* to use in either a group situation or for your own private study.

Whatever form your study might take, we have prayerfully prepared our notes from each of the nine parts*, reflecting on both what Derek has said during the video, as well as including extracts taken from Derek's books on similar subjects. Some of the questions are straight forward but many are not, encouraging you to seek out for yourself exactly what God is saying to you.

We have endeavoured to make the study as flexible as possible to suit your needs, so that if you only have a short time available after viewing the video, you can get straight into the questions. If you have longer, we would suggest you explore the extra material before answering the questions.

The following are suggestions to help you in your group discussions.

1 Starting with yourself

Prepare yourself by viewing the part of the video you are to discuss, ahead of time. Take time to consider your response to what you have seen and heard and make some notes of your own.

2 About others

Allow people to express their reactions. If nobody wants to be the first to speak, you might ask: What particularly impressed you tonight?

3 Be flexible

Make room for the Holy Spirit to guide you and ask for His help; it isn't important to adhere strictly to the questions provided. Remember – it is good to be able to steer people towards the Scriptures rather than personal viewpoints, and this is the reason why we have concluded each part with God's Word. Derek said, 'Your attitude towards God's Word determines your relationship with God' and if you make studying God's Word a priority, long after you have finished working your way through the Scriptures in this booklet, you will enjoy a closer relationship with God.

** Please note that each part of the video is equal to two sections of the Study Guide*

Part One

The Journey Begins

My Grandmother's Prayers

Derek speaks fondly of his family; in particular he mentions his grandparents, with whom he had a very good relationship. He said:

I came to realise later that both my grandmother and my grandfather were sincere believers . . . I remember I would burst into my grandmother's bedroom at about 7 o'clock in the evening and she was always on her knees praying. I am sure she was praying for her grandson who had all sorts of potential problems. In fact I have to say that one of the great influences in my life was my grandmother's prayers.

Questions to ponder and discuss

1. How important do you think it is to pray for our children?
2. Have the prayers of your family had an effect on your life?
3. How can we 'train up a child in the way he should go'?
4. What does Paul tell us in his letter to the Philippians that we will receive if we pray and trust God?
5. Whose help do we need to pray for when we do not know how to pray? (See page 8.)
6. How should we respond to God's warning in Hosea 4:6?

Derek stresses the importance of giving children our time, in *God's Remedy for Rejection*:

If you talk to many children today who are bitter and rebellious toward their parents, they will tell you this, 'Our parents gave us clothes and an education and a car and a swimming pool, but they never gave us time. They never gave us themselves.'

This, I think, is one reason for the bitter reaction we saw in the 1960s of young people against the older generations. It was a reaction against loveless materialism. Many of those young people who became so bitter and rebellious were from rather privileged, wealthy homes. They had been given everything except love, which was the thing they wanted and needed most.

Derek also teaches in *Fatherhood*:

In these last two decades, we have seen millions of children go into various kinds of satanic captivity—to drugs, illicit sex, the occult and various types of cults. That is captivity, just as surely as if an invading alien army had come into the country and carried them off prisoner. Why did these millions of children go into captivity? The answer is given there in the Scriptures. Because their fathers failed in their responsibilities. The primary responsibility for that state of affairs in modern society rests at the door of the fathers.

We hear a lot about juvenile delinquents. There are hardly any juvenile delinquents until there are first adult delinquents. It takes adult delinquents to bring forth juvenile delinquents.

I pointed out earlier that one of the father's responsibilities to his family was that a priest. In Malachi 2:7, the Lord states what is required of a priest:

> For one priest's lips should seek the law at his mouth; for He is a messenger of the Lord of hosts.
> *Malachi 2:7 KJV*

Derek encourages us to intercede for our children in *Husbands and Fathers*:

Let's look at a picture of a man in the Old Testament, Job, who was a model as priest of his family. We read at the opening of the book that Job was a perfect and upright man before God. One day each week his seven sons and three daughters met in the house of one of his sons for feasting and fellowship. At the end of each week Job got up early in the morning and offered sacrifices on behalf of all his children, saying, 'It may be that they have failed and are not right with God. I will make a sacrifice on their behalf.'

When Job offered a sacrifice for his children, he was claiming the benefits of the sacrifice on their behalf. That is a picture of intercession: claiming the benefits of a sacrifice on behalf of those for whom you are praying.

Our sacrifice at this point in history, of course, is the sacrifice of Jesus on the Cross. Intercession for our children, then, involves claiming the benefits of Christ's death on their behalf.

Every father, as priest of his family, needs to learn a lesson from Job. None of us has any guarantee that some unforeseen tragedy or disaster will not, in one instant, carry one or more of the members of our family out of time into eternity. Every father is responsible before God, therefore, to maintain day-to-day intercession for his whole household. We must also guard against the mistake of looking for the answers to our prayers only on earth and in the present age. Only in eternity shall we know the full outworking of our prayers.

The Bible tells us:

Be anxious for nothing, but in everything by prayer and supplication, with thanksgiving, let your requests be made known to God; and the peace of God which surpasses all understanding, will guard your hearts and minds through Christ Jesus.
Philippians 4:6-7

Likewise the Spirit also helps in our weaknesses. For we do not know what we should pray for as we ought, but the Spirit Himself makes intercession for us with groanings which cannot be uttered.
Romans 8:26-27

My people are destroyed for lack of knowledge. Because you have rejected knowledge, I also will reject you from being priest for Me; because you have forgotten the law of your God, I also will forget your children.
Hosea 4:6

Train up a child in the way he should go,
And when he is old he will not depart from it.
Proverbs 22:6

The Dissatisfaction of Youth

As a young man, Derek felt dissatisfied with the status quo . . .

To look back to my late teens, I would have to say I was a hippy before there were hippies and much of the motivation of the hippies and those who follow them, was my motivation.

I was dissatisfied with the status quo. I couldn't improve it but I didn't want to become a part of it. And being a philosopher, it is an open door to all sorts of things. I became interested in Indian philosophies.

Questions to ponder and discuss

1. Can you identify with Derek when he said he couldn't 'accept the status quo'? When have you felt this way?
2. What are the dangers of searching around for answers, in various philosophies?
3. How can we help young people find the truth?

Describing this time in his life, Derek tells us in *Pages from My Life's Book* that he was 'an idealist' and that the frustrations of life led him to drink:

Finding that philosophy did not have a very clear or positive answer, I turned to Oriental cults and systems such as are extremely fashionable in our contemporary society . . . I turned to Yoga, to Theosophy, and even to Voodoo . . . I practised meditational and positional yoga. But again I ended up in disillusionment. I had a certain kind of supernatural experience, but it did not make me happy.

In fact, it was followed by a grey depression that settled around me. When I could not stand the tension between the ideal and the actual any longer, a friend and I would listen to classical music and drink whisky. When we had finished one bottle, we would often go on to the second.

. . . Looking back, I can say about that period in my life that I achieved academic success . . . I had a certain reputation. I had written a dissertation of Plato's method of definition and its evolution. I knew a lot of long words and phrases and had tried a lot of different things. But looking back, I would have to admit I was confused and frustrated, disappointed and disillusioned, and did not know where to find the answer.

The Bible tells us:

Jesus said: I am the way, the truth and the life. No one comes to the Father except through me.
John 14:6

Jesus said: I am the light of the world. He who follows Me shall not walk in darkness, but have the light of life.
John 8:12

And do not be conformed to this world, but be transformed by the renewing of your mind, that you may prove what is that good and acceptable and perfect will of God.
Romans 12:1-2

The fear of the Lord is the beginning of knowledge,
But fools despise wisdom and instruction.
Proverbs 1:7

Hear, my children, the instruction of a father,
And give attention to know understanding;
For I give you good doctrine:

Do not forsake my law.
When I was my father's son,
Tender and the only one in the sight of my mother,
He also taught me, and said to me:
'Let your heart retain my words;
Keep my commands, and live,
Get wisdom! Get understanding!
Do not forget, nor turn away from the words of my mouth,
Do not forsake her, and she will preserve you;
Love her, and she will keep you.
Wisdom is the principal thing;
Therefore get wisdom,
And in all your getting, get understanding.
Exalt her, and she will promote you;
She will bring you honour, when you embrace her.
She will place on your head an ornament of grace;
A crown of glory she will deliver to you.'
Proverbs 4:1-9

Apply your heart to instruction,
And your ears to words of knowledge.
Proverbs 23:12

Part Two

War and Salvation

Praying for the Sick

Derek described meeting a couple who had invited him back for supper after a meeting. The wife told Derek that her husband had tuberculosis in one lung and that she had prayed every day for ten years for her husband to be healed. Derek thought, 'Could anybody pray about anything every day for ten years?'

But the woman went on to say, 'At the end of ten years, I was praying alone in a room. My husband was in the bedroom, sitting up in bed, propped up on the pillows, coughing up blood. As I was praying, an audible voice spoke to me and said, 'Claim it!' and I answered out loud, 'Lord, I claim it now!'

When she said that, her husband in the bed in the other room was healed of tuberculosis. When he went back to the doctor to be examined, the doctor hold him that the lung that had been affected was stronger than the lung that had never been affected.

Questions to ponder and discuss

1. Should we always pray for the sick to be healed?
2. What should we do when someone says, 'You can pray for me but I don't think it will work'?
3. What is the root cause of all human suffering? (1 John 3:8)
4. What two things does God's Word give us? (Proverbs 4:20-22)

Derek teaches us about healing from the *Self Study Bible Course*:

Healing for our bodies from God comes to us through hearing and believing God's Word, and through allowing God's Spirit to fill our bodies with the resurrection life of Christ. Not only may we receive healing for our own bodies in this way, but we may also offer healing and deliverance to others in the name of Jesus. Two main ways in which we may do this are by laying our hands on the sick and praying for them, or by getting believing church elders to anoint them with oil in the name of the Lord. If we act in faith in this way, God will work with us and confirm the truth of His Word by miracles of healing and deliverance.

Derek tells us more about healing in his book, *God's Medicine Bottle*:

One day I came across some verses in the book of Proverbs which I learned to call 'God's Medicine Bottle'. I'm quoting from the King James version which was the version that I was reading in those days and which is extremely vivid and forceful:

My son, attend to my words; incline thine ear unto my sayings. Let them not depart from thine eyes; keep them in the midst of thine heart. For they are life unto those that find them, and health to all their flesh.
Proverbs 4:20–22 KJV

It was that last phrase, 'health to all their flesh,' that caught my attention. I understood that 'all their flesh' meant the total physical body, which is the way more modern versions translate it. I reasoned with myself, 'Health! If I have health in my whole body, then I have no room anywhere for sickness. That is what God is promising me.'

The Bible tells us:

He will bless your bread and water. And I will take sickness away from the midst of you.
Exodus 23:25

Surely He has borne our griefs
And carried our sorrows;
Yet we esteemed Him stricken,
Smitten by God, and afflicted.
But He was wounded for our transgressions,
He was bruised for our iniquities;
The chastisement for our peace was upon Him,
And by His stripes we are healed.
Isaiah 53:4-5

My son, give attention to my words;
Incline your ear to my sayings.
Do not let them depart from your eyes;
Keep them in the midst of your heart;
For they are life to those who find them,
And health to all their flesh.
Proverbs 4:20-22

And Jesus went about all Galilee, teaching in their synagogues, preaching the gospel of the kingdom, and healing all kinds of sickness and all kinds of disease among the people.
Matthew 4:23

And these signs will follow those who believe:
In My name they will cast out demons; they will speak with new tongues; they will take up serpents: and if they drink anything deadly, it will by no means hurt them; they will lay hands on the sick and they will recover.
Mark 16:17-18

For this purpose the Son of God was manifested, that He might destroy the works of the devil.
1 John 3:8

An Encounter with the Holy Spirit

After Derek had met the author of his black leather Bible, he was totally changed. He said that since that time, he has never doubted that Jesus is alive:

I was a different person. The night before I hadn't known how to pray, what to say, or to whom to pray. Now I discovered that I was praying all the time. I made no effort, instead each breath was a prayer. I remember going to a tap to draw water to drink, but I could not drink until I had thanked God for it. Also I had been a habitual blasphemer, now the words didn't come out.

The next evening I went to go for my usual drink, intending to walk in, but my legs locked! And no matter how hard I tried, I could not get them to carry my body into that pub! At first I felt indignant . . . then I realised I wasn't the least bit interested. I went back to read my Bible and opened it up to the Psalms where it says,

When the Lord brought back the captivity of Zion,
We were like those who dream.
Then our mouth was filled with laughter,
And our tongue with singing.
Psalm 126:1-3

I said to myself: 'That's what's happened to me!' I wasn't laughing, my mouth was filled with laughter! I came into a relationship with the Bible which I've had ever since. God speaks to me. It's not just theology or history. It's the Living Word. It's God the Father speaking to His child and that really was a total turning point in my life.

Questions to ponder and discuss

1. What changes should we look for when someone is Spirit-filled?
2. Who is the true author of the Scriptures, both Old and New Testaments?
3. How does God speak to you?

Derek teaches us on the Holy Spirit from *The Holy Spirit In You*:

The revealing of the Scripture was an immediate result on the Day of Pentecost. When the Holy Spirit fell, the unbelieving crowd said, 'They're drunk.' But Peter stood up and said the following:

> These men are not drunk, as you suppose. It's only nine in the morning! No, this is what was spoken by the prophet Joel.
> *Acts 2:15-16 NIV*

Up to that time, Peter had no understanding of the prophecy of Joel. In fact, he had a very limited understanding even of the teaching of Jesus. But the moment the Holy Spirit came, the Bible made sense for him in a totally new way because the author was there to interpret.

The Bible tells us:

But the Helper, the Holy Spirit, whom the Father will send in My name, He will teach you all things, and bring to your remembrance all things that I said to you.
John 14:26

However, when He, the Spirit of truth, has come, He will guide you into all truth; for He will not speak on His own authority, but whatever He hears He will speak; and He will tell you things to come. He will glorify Me, for He will take of what is Mine and declare it to you.
John 16:13-14

All Scripture is God-breathed and is useful for teaching, rebuking, correcting and training in righteousness.
2 Timothy 3:16 NIV

Part Three

In the Desert

The Power of Proclaiming God's Word

When Derek was serving in the army, he describes how he prayed for victory during a particularly difficult time of retreat. He was disappointed in the leaders and He felt God give him this prayer to proclaim: 'Lord, give us leaders for your glory to give us victory.' He prayed this prayer faithfully until He saw God's miraculous intervention. Churchill appointed Montgomery – who was the son of an evangelical Anglican bishop – as the new commander-in-chief. He was a man who fulfilled God's two requirements in a leader of men. He was just and God-fearing; a man of tremendous discipline. Derek tells us that after a few months, Montgomery had instilled a totally new sense of discipline in his officers and restored the confidence of the men in their leaders.

. . . Then the main battle of El Alamein was fought. It was the first major allied victory in the entire war up to that time . . . Two or three days after the battle, I found myself in the desert a few miles behind the Advancing Allied forces. A small portable radio beside me on the tailboard of a military truck was relaying a news commentator's description of the scene at Montgomery's headquarters as he had witnessed it on the eve of the battle.

Derek recalled how Montgomery publicly called his officers and men to prayer, saying:

'Let us ask the Lord, mighty in battle, to give us the victory.'

. . . And when he said that, heaven's electricity went through me from the crown of my head to the soles of my feet!

God said: 'That's the answer to your prayer!' I knew from that moment on that God can intervene in history if we know how to pray.

(This story can be found in *Shaping History Through Prayer and Fasting.*)

Questions to ponder and discuss

1. Can you recall a difficult situation where you have asked God to intervene? What was the outcome?
2. Have you an issue in your life that needs God's breakthrough? Ask God to show you how to pray.
3. Should we pray for leaders in government and areas of important responsibility on a regular basis?
4. What can we be confident of if we pray in the will of God?

Derek teaches us how to pray powerfully by proclaiming the Word of God in *The Power of Proclamation*:

Tremendous power is released through proclaiming the Word of God . . . The word 'to proclaim' comes from a Latin word which means to 'shout forth' . For us, as believers in the Bible, confession means that we say the same with our mouths as God has already said in His Word. We make the words of our mouth agree with the Word of God. In that way we line ourselves up to receive the full backing and authority of Jesus.

Here are some Scriptures that will encourage and help you. One of my favourites is a combination of Daniel 2:20-22 and Daniel 4:34-35. The first words were spoken by Daniel and the second by Nebuchadnezzar but the message is the same.

> Blessed be the name of God for ever and ever,
> For wisdom and might are His.
> And He changes the times and the seasons;
> He removes kings and raises up kings;
> He gives wisdom to the wise
> And knowledge to those who
> have understanding.
> He reveals deep and secret things;
> He knows what is in the darkness
> And the light dwells with Him.
> For His dominion is an everlasting dominion,
> And His kingdom is from generation to generation.
> All the inhabitants of the earth are reputed as nothing;
> He does according to His will in the army of heaven
> and among the inhabitants of the earth.
> No one can restrain His hand or say to Him,
> 'What have you done?'

Remember that the second section of those words came from a ruler who not long before that had been an unbeliever. That should encourage us that God can indeed change the hearts of evil rulers if we learn how to pray.

The Bible tells us:

> If my people who are called by my name will humble themselves, and pray and seek my face and turn from their wicked ways, then will I hear from heaven, and will forgive their sin and will heal their land.
> *2 Chronicles 7:14*

Therefore I tell you, whatever you ask for in prayer, believe that you have received it, and it will be yours.
Mark 11:24 NIV

Now this is the confidence that we have in Him, that if we ask anything according to His will, He hears us. And if we know that He hears us, whatever we ask, we know that we have the petitions that we have asked of Him.
1 John 5:14-15

The Atoning Work of Calvary

When Derek was suffering from his debilitating skin disease, he was visited by the lady brigadier, Mrs Ross, from the Salvation Army along with her co-worker, a young woman from Oklahoma. Mrs Ross had heard there was a young soldier who was sick and had come to pray for him, persuading a New Zealand soldier to drive them some fifty miles to get there. This is how Derek recalled what happened after they started to pray and the young American began to speak in tongues.

We began to pray and this young woman beside me began to vibrate . . . and then I started to vibrate and then everyone in the car began to vibrate and then the car itself began to vibrate – and the engine was not running and I was aware that God was doing something.

The young woman spoke in another language and then gave the interpretation. I do not remember all that she said, but a certain passage is as fresh for me today as it was in 1943:

'Consider the work of Calvary: a perfect work, perfect in every respect, perfect in every aspect.'

God had shown me the place to look for an answer – what He called 'the work of Calvary', the perfect sacrifice – the atoning sacrifice of

Jesus on the Cross. And over the years I've come to see that what Jesus did for me on the Cross was the perfect sacrifice, giving us forgiveness from sin, cleansing from sin and healing for our physical bodies.

Questions to ponder and discuss

1. What do you understand by 'the work of the Cross'?
2. What did Jesus bear for our forgiveness?
3. What other afflictions did He bear for us and what do we receive?
4. How do we appropriate practically what God has done for us through the Cross?

Derek teaches us from *Atonement – Your Appointment with God*:

The work of the Cross is 'perfect in every respect, perfect in every aspect.' It matters not from what point of view you look at the Cross. It is perfect. Nothing has been omitted. 'All things that pertain to life and godliness' (2 Peter 1:3) – and that covers just about everything! – are provided for in the sacrificial death of Jesus on the Cross. Everything you will ever need in time and eternity, whether spiritual or physical, financial or material, emotional or relational, has been provided by that one sacrifice. 'He has perfected forever those who are being sanctified' (Hebrews 10:14). Notice again that word 'perfected'. So I set myself to understand what God did for me through Jesus on the Cross. I began to see that on the Cross Jesus bore not only my sins but also my sicknesses and pains, so that by His wounds I was healed. The message of Isaiah 53:4-5 was inescapable.

The Bible tells us:

Surely He has borne our griefs (literally, sicknesses) and carried our sorrows (literally, pains); yet we esteemed Him stricken, smitten by God and afflicted. But He was wounded for our transgressions, He was bruised for our iniquities; the chastisement for our peace was upon Him, and by His stripes (or wounds) we are healed.
Isaiah 53:4-5

For by one offering He has perfected forever those who are being sanctified. But the Holy Spirit also witnesses to us; for after He had said before,

'This is the covenant that I will make with them after those days, says the Lord: I will put My laws into their hearts, and in their minds I will write them.' Then He adds,

'Their sins and their lawless deeds I will remember no more.'

Now where there is remission of these, there is no longer an offering for sin.

Therefore, brethren, having boldness, to enter the Holiest by the blood of Jesus, by a new and living way which He consecrated for us, through the veil, that is, His flesh, and having a High Priest over the house of God, let us draw near with a true heart in full assurance of faith, having our hearts sprinkled from an evil conscience and our bodies washed with pure water. Let us hold fast the confession of our hope without wavering, for He who promised is faithful.
Hebrews 10:14-23

Therefore, having been justified by faith, we have peace with God through our Lord Jesus Christ.
Romans 5:1

For it pleased the Father that in Him all the fullness (of God) should dwell, and by Him to reconcile all things to Himself, by Him, whether things on earth or things in heaven, having made peace through the blood of His Cross. And you, who once were alienated and enemies in your mind by wicked works, yet now He has reconciled in the body of His flesh through death, to present you holy, and blameless, and above reproach in His sight.
Colossians 1:19-22

In (Jesus) we have redemption through His blood, the forgiveness of sins, according to the riches of His grace.
Ephesians 1:7

Part Four

Appointment in Jerusalem

Living the Life of Faith

After the Sudan, Derek was sent to Palestine where he was posted to Qiryat Motzkia on the shore of the Mediterranean. Derek tells us:

I had heard about a Danish missionary who had a children's home in a small Arab village. I was told, 'If you want a blessing go to the children's home.'

I arrived and found Lydia with eight small girls. I was impressed by the sense of peace which was a very, very rare thing in Israel.

One of Derek's daughters, Titva said:
'We were brought up with prayer and faith. I remember when I was very young, we had no food and Mummy said, "Come on girls, kneel down." So we all had to kneel down and ask for food . . . In the morning we opened the door and there was a basket of eggs and some milk. We never knew who bought it . . . We were brought up to believe God will supply all our needs and He did and He is still doing it, even now.'

Questions to ponder and discuss

1. Who do you know that you could send others to, who would be a blessing? Discuss why.
2. How would you describe 'faith in God'?
3. Can you relate to Titva's experience of relying on God for essential provision? If so, how do you think this has affected your faith levels?

Derek challenges us in *Who Cares for Orphans, Widows, the Poor and Oppressed*:

Whom is Jesus concerned about? The poor, the meek, the oppressed, the people that don't get a fair deal.

Personally, I come from a privileged level of society in Britain. I'm not speaking about what I didn't get because I got a lot more than I should have. But I have come to realise that most of the people in this country are not really getting what they should. That may shock you, but I find it is true. The basic reason for this is human selfishness. Everybody cares for themselves. Do you know you can be Pentecostal and very selfish? You can speak in tongues and be very self-centred, very concerned about yourself. I believe in speaking in tongues; I speak in tongues every day. But that's not a substitute for my character.
Isaiah 58 is a passage that David Wilkerson calls, 'the key to continuing revival.' The record of his ministry probably justifies his claim.

Derek instructs us how to build our faith through the Scriptures in *Thanksgiving, Praise and Worship*:

These verses based on Colossians 3 show us how to be a blessing and 'let the peace of God rule in our hearts'.

> As the elect of God, holy and beloved, we put on tender mercies, kindness, humbleness of mind, meekness, long-suffering; bearing with one another, and forgiving one another, if anyone has a complaint against another. Even as Christ forgave us, so we

also must do. But above all these things we put on love, which is the bond of perfection. We let the peace of God rule in our hearts, to which also we were called in one body, and we are thankful. We let the Word of Christ dwell in us richly in all wisdom, teaching and admonishing one another in psalms and hymns and spiritual songs, singing with grace in our hearts to the Lord. And whatever we do in word or deed, we do all in the name of the Lord Jesus, giving thanks to God the Father through Him.

Derek teaches us about faith from *Foundations For Christian Living*:

But without faith it is impossible to please Him (God), for He who comes to God must believe that He is, and that He is a rewarder of those who diligently seek Him.
Hebrews 11:6

Notice the two phrases: 'without faith it is impossible to please God,' and 'he who comes to God must believe.' We see from these that faith is the indispensable condition for approaching God and for pleasing God.

The just shall live by his faith.
Habakkuk 2:4

Though so short and so simple, the scope of this sentence, 'The just shall live by faith', is immense. The word 'live' covers almost every conceivable condition or act of any sentient being. It covers all areas of the human personality and experience in every conceivable aspect – the spiritual, the mental, the physical, the material. It covers the widest possible range of activities – such as breathing, thinking, speaking, eating, sleeping, working and so on.

The Scripture teaches that, for any person to be accepted as righteous by God, all these activities within that person must be motivated and controlled by the one great principle of faith.

True faith causes man to acknowledge his own limitations. True faith distinguishes between those things which are within the province of man and those which are within the province of God.

Someone has stated the relationship between man's part and God's part in the life of faith as follows: 'You do the simple thing; God will do the complicated thing. You do the small thing; God will do the great thing. You do the possible thing; God will do the impossible thing.'

The Bible tells us:

> But Jesus looked at them and said to them, 'With men this is impossible, but with God all things are possible.'
> *Matthew 19:26*

> Jesus said to him, 'If you believe, all things are possible to him who believes.'
> *Mark 9:23*

> Every place that the sole of your foot will tread upon I have given you.
> *Joshua 1:3*

> Commit your way to the Lord,
> Trust also in Him,
> And He shall bring it to pass.
> *Psalm 37:5*

Allowing God to Guide Our Lives

As we know from the Scriptures, God's ways are often very different to ours. Marrying Lydia, Derek's first wife, when she was born in the same year as Derek's mother, must have seemed strange to many. Certainly Lydia needed some convincing! God told Derek, 'I have joined you together in the same yoke and in the same harness.'

Derek said:
I felt God wanted me to be part of that children's home which is the most improbable destination for a person with my background . . . God does extraordinary things, if you allow Him to do them! One advantage I had is that I was pretty prepared to let God do some extraordinary things which otherwise He would not have done. Obviously He would not have forced it on me and I understand now . . . 'the same yoke' meant my marriage and the 'harness' was serving the Lord together. For thirty years we served the Lord together . . . I was the instrument of God to save the life of the family for probably, without me, they would have been massacred by Arabs.

Questions to ponder and discuss

1. Are you prepared to let God do something extraordinary in your life?
2. How easy is it for you to 'Trust in the Lord . . . and not lean on your own understanding'? Discuss.
3. Does your daily life lack victory or fruitfulness? What can you do about this?

Derek teaches us about doing the right thing at the right time in his book, *Foundations for Christian Living*:

In order to enjoy success and the blessing of God, we must do the right thing at the right time, and we must carry out the right purpose at the right season. When God says, 'Now,' it is vain for man to say, 'Later.' And when God says, 'Later,' it is vain for man to say, 'Now.'

It is the God-appointed ministry of the Holy Spirit to reveal to the Church not merely the right thing or the right purpose, but also the right time and the right season. Many sincere and well-meaning Christians who have not learned to make room for the guidance of the Holy Spirit encounter continual frustration in their lives simply through seeking to do the right thing at the wrong time and to carry out the right purpose at the wrong season. In this connection, the prophet Isaiah poses a very searching question.

> Who has directed the Spirit of the Lord,
> Or as His counsellor has taught Him?
> *Isaiah 40:13*

Yet this is just what many Christians are doing today: They are seeking to direct the Spirit of the Lord and to act as counsellor to the Holy Spirit. They plan their own activities, conduct their own services and then tell the Holy Spirit just what, when and how they expect Him to bless. In how many congregations today is there any real room left for the Holy Spirit either to direct or to intervene?

The Bible tells us:

> For my thoughts are not your thoughts,
> Nor are your ways My ways, says the Lord.
> For as the heavens are higher than the earth,
> So are My ways higher than your ways,
> And My thoughts than your thoughts.
> *Isaiah 55:8-9*

> Trust in the Lord with all your heart,
> And lean not on your own understanding;
> In all your ways acknowledge Him,
> And He shall direct your paths.
> *Proverbs 3:5-6*

> For as many as are led by the spirit of God, these are the sons of God.
> *Romans 8:14*

Part Five

Escape from Jerusalem

God's Protection

God protects and keeps us safe in times of trouble. Derek describes how God protected his family when full-scale fighting broke out in Jerusalem. Their home was just a quarter of a mile from the front line. Lydia had prayed, 'Lord paralyse the Arabs!' Derek said that their backyard was taken over by the Haganah – the volunteer Jewish defence force that later developed into the official Israeli army. An observation post under the command of a young man named Phinehas was located in the yard.

Derek tells us:

Because of this, we became quite well acquainted with a number of the young Jewish people who manned the post. Early in June 1948, the United Nations succeeded in imposing a four-week cease-fire and there was a temporary lull in the fighting. One day during the cease-fire, some of our young Jewish friends were sitting in our living room talking, and a young man said, 'There's something we can't understand. We go into an area where the Arabs are – they outnumber us ten to one and are much better armed than we are – yet at times, they seem powerless to do anything against us. It's as if they are paralysed!'

Questions to ponder and discuss

1. What can we learn from Derek's account of facing a dangerous situation?
2 What can we learn from David's life about God's protection from reading the Psalms?

Derek teaches us from Psalm 35:1-3 in *Through the Psalms with Derek Prince*:

Contend, O Lord, with those who contend with me;
fight against those who fight against me.
Take up shield and buckler;
arise and come to my aid.
Brandish spear and block the way
against those who pursue me.
Say to my soul,
'I am your salvation.'

That was a prayer of David in a time of deep distress. He found himself surrounded by enemies pressing in against him and he saw no way to keep them out. He had exhausted his own strength and his own resources. So he cried out to the Lord: 'Take Your stand against my enemies. Interpose Yourself between me and them.' David saw that he needed more than weapons; he needed God in His own Person to be his defence.

David's prayer was answered at the time in a way that met his immediate need, but that was not the end. The final, conclusive answer to David's prayer came a thousand years later through David's greater Son, the Lord Jesus Christ. On the Cross Jesus did just what David had cried out for. Jesus interposed Himself; He blocked the way against every enemy of our souls. By His atoning death He cancelled every claim and silenced every accusation of Satan. He set a limit to Satan's territory. He created a boundary that Satan cannot pass over.

If you find yourself, like David, harassed by enemies of your soul too strong and cunning for you, then accept for yourself the answer to David's prayer. Take refuge behind the Cross of Jesus, and hear Him say to your soul, 'I am your salvation.'

The Bible tells us:

The Lord will keep you from all harm –
He will watch over your life;
The Lord will watch over your coming and going both now and forevermore.
Psalms 121:7-8

Have I not commanded you? Be strong and of good courage; do not be afraid, nor be dismayed, for the Lord your God is with you wherever you go.
Joshua 1:9

My flesh and my heart may fail;
But God is the strength of my heart
and my portion forever.
Psalm 73:26

I shall not die, but live,
And declare the works of the Lord.
Psalm 118:17

God's Provision

Derek and Lydia became caught up in the tumultuous train of events that proved to be the labour pains of the State of Israel. Their lives were frequently in danger and they had to move home four times – twice at night. War and famine were all around them but Derek said, 'God protected and provided for us in ways that continually amazed us.'

When the family needed to move from Ramallah to Jerusalem, this is what happened:

We made many attempts by bus to Jerusalem but we were unsuccessful. Eventually I said to Lydia, 'Look if God wants us to move to Jerusalem, God can send someone to our door in Ramallah,' which was a rather foolish thing to say. But within a week an Assyrian from

Bethlehem turned up on our doorstep and said 'We have just finished building a house in Jerusalem, would like you to rent it?'

Another example of God's provision was having an adequate food supply. Derek tells us that despite a shortage of food, his family did not go short as the previous tenants had left boxes of canned goods. Later as they were leaving on the last convoy out of Jerusalem, the family sold the rest of the food to provide the money needed for their travel to England.

Questions to ponder and discuss

1 What can we learn about God's provision from Derek's life?
2. When you are in need, what do you do? Search out the Scriptures on God's provision.

Derek teaches us about God's provision in *Receiving God's Best*:

. . . There is a tremendous statement made by Jesus in John 10:29 (NRSV): 'What my Father has given me is greater than all.' This is the marginal version in more than one of the modern translations. I have looked at the original Greek text and believe this is the best authenticated original text.

'What my father has given me is greater than all!' That is a breathtaking statement! Ultimately the most important and irresistible thing in the universe, the one thing that is absolutely sure, settled, and cannot be challenged or overthrown, is the thing that the Father has given. That is greater than all. It is something that no power of hell, or demons or evil rulers can ever undo, overthrow, or unsettle.

It was characteristic of Jesus that He never wanted anything except what the Father had given. There was no force that could ever take from Jesus what the Father had given. What is true of Him is true, in like measure, of you and me. What the Father has given to you and me is greater than all. Do not get nervous or uptight about the opposition. The very fact that you get uptight is evidence that you are really not moving into what the Father has given you. If you know the Father has given it to you, you can smile at the opposition. It is absolutely guaranteed. The supreme factor in the course of the universe is what God the Father has given.

These are the words of Jesus from the Sermon on the Mount:

> Blessed are meek, for they will inherit the earth.
> *Matthew 5:5*

The Bible also tells us:

> And God is able to make all grace abound toward you, that you, always having all sufficiency in all things, may have an abundance for every good work.
> *2 Corinthians 9:8*

> Now to Him who is able to do exceedingly abundantly above all that we ask or think, according to the power that works in us, to Him be glory in the church by Christ Jesus to all generations, forever and ever. Amen.
> *Ephesians 3:20-21*

> So I say to you, ask, and it will be given to you; seek, and you will find; knock, and it will be opened to you. For everyone who receives, and he who seeks finds, and to him who knocks it will be opened.
> *Luke 11:9*

> If you ask anything in My name, I will do it.
> *John 14:14*

Part Six

Refugees and Africa

Testing Times

Derek mentions that the family went through some real testing times when they came to England. They had a large family and only a very small income.

In London we were really refugees. It is hard to be a refugee but to be a refugee in your own country is very hard. We went through some real tests. Many people were very kind to us, some Christians took us in, some didn't . . .

Questions to ponder and discuss

1. Derek tells us that we will all be tested. What has been your experience of being tested by God?

2. What does 'taking up the cross daily' mean to you? How have you denied yourself?

3. When we are going through a trial, what should we be careful to avoid? See Exodus 15:22-24.

4. Can you explain the difference between God's testing and temptation? Discuss.

Derek teaches us about testing in *Life's Bitter Pool* from Exodus 15:22–24 (NIV):

Then Moses led Israel from the Red Sea and they went into the Desert of Shur. For three days they travelled in the desert without finding water. When they came to Marah, they could not drink its water because it was bitter. (That is why the place is called Marah.) *In Hebrew, 'Marah' is the word for bitter.* So the people grumbled against Moses, saying, 'What are we to drink?'

. . . You see, the question in our lives is not whether we will experience testing, but only how we will respond to the testing. The testing there at Marah exposes an area in the character of the Israelites that needed to be dealt with; an area that was expressed in grumbling.

Derek also teaches from Luke 9:23 (KJV) in *The Grace of Yielding*:

And he said to them all, if any man will come after me *(this is absolutely universal)*, let him deny himself, and take up his cross daily, and follow me.

What is the first thing you do when you decide to follow Jesus? The first step. Let him do what? Deny himself. You cannot begin to follow Jesus until you make that decision. And then it goes on, 'And take up his cross daily.'

I never liked that word 'daily'. For a long time I steered around that verse in Luke 9, because I knew another verse where it doesn't put the 'daily' in . . . At that time my theology and my teaching was all built on a once-and-for-all experience of the Cross. If you use the opportunity, you have a victorious day. If you lose the opportunity, you have a day of defeat.

But what is your cross? I heard a fellow preacher say it this way: 'Your cross is where your will and the will of God cross.' Your cross is the thing on which you can die. It's the place where you can lay down your life. When Jesus went to the Cross He said, 'No man taketh my life from me. I have power to lay it down, I have power to take it up'. (John 10:18) In this sense, no one will take your life from you. If you don't voluntarily lay it down, you'll still be in control of it.

Many, many times you and I come to a situation in the day where God's will and our will cross. We have to see that as a God-given opportunity – not a disaster, but an opportunity.

The Bible tells us:

We consider it pure joy, whenever we face trials of many kinds, because we know that the testing of our faith develops perseverance. But we must let perseverance finish its work so that we may be mature and complete, not lacking anything.
James 1:2-4 NIV

Blessed is the man who trusts in the Lord,
whose confidence is in him.
He will be like a tree planted by the water
that sends out its roots by the stream.
It does not fear when heat comes;
It has no worries in a year of drought
and never fails to bear fruit.
Jeremiah 17:7-8 NIV

I know how to be abased, and I know how to abound. Everywhere and in all things I have learned both to

be full and to be hungry, both to abound and to suffer need. I can do all things through Christ who strengthens me.
Philippians 4:12-13

The Power of God

Derek describes his home with its large upper room which he used for his congregation. God came with power to transform the lives of the people.

There were a few people with a real hunger for God but most of the people were callous and indifferent and disillusioned because we'd won a war but lost so much. We'd won very little from the war. We would preach at Speaker's Corner in Marble Arch and invite them back to 77 Westbourne Grove.

. . . During that time many people came to the Lord, many were baptised in the Holy Spirit, some received miraculous healings, we never grew to a large number of people but God was at work . . . One evening a man came in on crutches – he had been previously injured – and he was healed. He threw away his crutches and there was such an outburst of praise and worship. The whole room was shaken by the power of God. This went on for about half an hour and some of our neighbours in the street said the next day – 'What happened to your building? It was shaking!'

Questions to ponder and discuss

1. Do you believe we have 'programmed the Holy Ghost out' of many of our churches? (See page 40.)
2. How can we be open to the Holy Spirit's guiding?

Derek teaches us about God's power in *Baptism in the Holy Spirit*:

Let me tell you of an incident that made a deep impression on me. I was speaking at a conference of the Full Gospel Businessmen in Spokane, Washington. It was held in a big hotel where several hundred people were present. I was teaching the afternoon Bible study, especially warning those in attendance about the dangers of fooling around with Pentecost. When I had come to the end of my message, I did not know what to do since they had no specified programme.

(Can you say 'Praise God'? Many Pentecostal people have programmed the Holy Ghost out of most Pentecostal churches. Did you know that? They do not allow room for the Holy Spirit to move, and they would be shocked if He did. They would have to stop doing something, which would upset them.)

Not knowing what else to do, I just stood there and was silent. Soon a lady began to sing in an unknown tongue. I would describe it as a kind of Gregorian chant. It so happened that the brother who was with me on the platform was a choir leader and quite an expert in music. When she had finished singing, he said, 'That was a very complicated melody.' We waited a little while, and a young man began to sing in English. He gave the interpretation of that song which was in an unknown tongue, singing in exactly the same melody. The words that he sang also fitted the melody. The man beside me said, 'He kept the melody perfectly.' In the course of the day, this happened twice.

The interesting part of this whole story is that I did something that we do not often do at these conventions.

We rarely ask others what their denomination affiliations are, since we are not concerned about particular labels. However, because it seemed to tie in so perfectly with the subject at hand, I made some inquiries about the denominational alliance of these two people. I discovered that the lady was a Lutheran and the young man was an Episcopalian. However, we were all one in Jesus Christ in the unity of the Holy Ghost.

Today the church of Jesus Christ faces two alternatives. On the one hand, we have union, and on the other, we have unity. I will not go as far as to say that these two are mutually exclusive. However, I close with the thought that man can make union, but only the Holy Ghost can make unity.

The Bible tells us:

And suddenly there came a sound from heaven,
as of a rushing mighty wind, and it filled the whole
house where they were sitting.
Acts 2:2

For by grace you have been saved through faith, and that not of yourselves; it is the gift of God, not of works, lest anyone should boast.
Ephesians 2:8-9

But the manifestation of the Spirit is given
to each one for the profit of all.
1 Corinthians 12:7

However, when He, the Spirit of truth, has come,
He will guide you into all truth; for He will not speak
on His own authority, but whatever He hears He will
speak; and He will tell you things to come.
He will glorify Me, for He will take of what is Mine
and declare it to you.
John 16:13-14

Part Seven

Deliverance

Christians Need Deliverance Too

In Seattle, Derek tells us he had a call from a Baptist pastor who said he had a woman who needed deliverance from evil spirits, and that the Lord had shown him that Derek and Lydia were to be the instruments of her deliverance. When the pastor arrived with an ordinary looking American woman Derek said:

I scanned her closely looking for some outward evidence of her strange spiritual condition – a wild look in her eyes, perhaps, or a metallic ring in her voice. But she seemed to be a perfectly ordinary, middle-class American housewife, somewhere in her middle thirties, I judged. She did not seem nervous or frightened.

Questions to ponder and discuss

1. As Christians, what do we need to do to be protected by the blood of Jesus? (See next page.)
2. What do you understand by 'deliverance'? Search out the Scriptures on this subject.
3. Expelling demons was a normal part of Jesus' ministry. Why do you think is this not the case today?

Derek teaches us about deliverance in *They Shall Expel Demons*:

Some Christians claim they are automatically protected from demonic attack by the blood of Jesus. God does indeed offer us total protection through the blood. But here again, this provision depends on our meeting His conditions.
The apostle Peter tells us we are the:

> . . . elect according to the foreknowledge of God the Father, in sanctification of the Spirit, for obedience and sprinkling of the blood of Jesus Christ.
> *1 Peter 1:2*

An obedient lifestyle is the condition for being protected by the blood of Jesus. His blood is not sprinkled on those who persist in disobedience. This is exemplified by the record of the first Passover in Egypt, when Moses told the Israelites:

> And you shall take a bunch of hyssop, dip it in the blood that is in the basin, and strike the lintel and the two doorposts with the blood that is in the basin. And none of you shall go out of the door of his house until morning.
> *Exodus 12:22*

The Israelites were protected not because they were Israelites, but because they obeyed God's instructions concerning the blood, and stayed inside their houses. They were on the right side of the blood. If the firstborn had gone out of their houses, they would have suffered the same fate as the Egyptians.

The same applies to us as Christians. Our protection from Satan does not depend solely on our being Christians, but on our obeying God's directions. The blood, as I said, does not protect those who continue in disobedience.

The apostle John wonderfully affirms the power of the blood of Jesus to deal with sin in our lives:

> But if we walk in the light as He is in the light, we have fellowship with one another, and the blood of Jesus Christ His Son cleanses us from all sin.
> *1 John 1:7*

The Bible also tells us:

> And He was preaching in the synagogues throughout all Galilee, and casting out demons.
> *Mark 1:39*

> Immediately the father of the child cried out and said with tears, 'Lord, I believe; help my unbelief!'
> *Mark 9:24–25*

> 'And these signs will follow those who believe: In My Name they will cast out demons; they will speak with new tongues.'
> *Mark 16:17*

Set Free

Derek described how the outcome of a young woman being set free was sad because she was too ashamed to be seen by the people who had witnessed her conduct. Derek asked himself:

This led me to search my own soul. What was I pastoring? A middle-class social club that meets on Sunday mornings? Or is it a place where people with real needs can come for help?

The events of that Sunday morning were like someone had thrown a big rock into the middle of a pond. First there was the big splash but after that the waves started to ripple out in all directions to the edge of the pond . . . and I cannot begin to explain . . . but people started to seek out Lydia and me.

Mostly they came to our home; a few came to the church – I have no idea how they knew our address. For weeks on end we hardly ever went to bed until about 2 a.m with people coming for deliverance.

Questions to ponder and discuss

1. What would you say to someone who believes Christians do not need deliverance? (See page 46.)
2. How can we learn more about this important ministry?
3. Derek said that he did not seek this ministry out for himself. Why do you think this is important?

Derek continues the story in his book *They Shall Expel Demons*:

I soon discovered, too, that proper instruction out of Scripture, is essential for effective deliverance. Before praying with people, I had to give them a sound biblical basis for what I was doing. In this way I built up faith in them to appropriate what Jesus had provided for them through His sacrificial death. Then, through our mutual faith, victory would be assured.

Meanwhile, God was leading me step by step from one new situation to another. Each successive situation revealed new aspects of the ministry – aspects I had to come to grips with. Then He led me on to the next situation – but only after I had 'graduated' from the previous one.

Evaluating all that had been happening, I realised God was not using the classroom method of a theological seminary to instruct me in the ministry of deliverance. He had me enrolled in a less prestigious school: the school of experience.

Also in *They Shall Expel Demons,* Derek commends us to look to Jesus:

To what kind of people, we might ask, was Jesus ministering in this way? Primarily observant Jews who met every Sabbath in the synagogue and spent the rest of the week caring for their families, tending their fields, fishing the sea and minding their shops. The people who received help from Jesus were mainly 'normal', respectable, religious people. Yet they were demonized. A demon had gained access to some area or areas of their personalities, and as a result they themselves were not in full control.

We need to remember that the moral and ethical code of Jewish people in Jesus' time was based on the Ten Commandments and the Law of Moses. This meant that most of them were probably living better lives than the majority of people in our contemporary Western society.

Undoubtedly there are many similar people to be found in the Christian community today – good, respectable, religious people who attend church and use all the right religious language, yet are like the observant Jews of Jesus' day. Some areas in their personalities have been invaded by demons and, as a result, they are not in full control. Surely they need deliverance just as much as the people to whom Jesus ministered!

The Bible tells us:

At evening, when the sun had set, they brought to Him all who were sick and those who were demon-possessed (demonized).

And the whole city was gathered together at the door. Then He healed many who were sick with various diseases, and cast out many demons; and He did not allow the demons to speak because they knew Him.
Mark 1:32-34

And He said to them, 'Go, tell that fox, "Behold, I cast out demons and perform cures today and tomorrow, and the third day I shall be perfected."'
Luke 13:32

But if I cast out demons by the Spirit of God, surely the kingdom of God has come upon you.
Matthew 12:28

Called Home

Derek describes Lydia's death with her family gathered around her.

Then in 1975 God called Lydia home quite suddenly, without any sickness. She was a very down-to-earth person down to the last moment. We all told her we loved her. Then she began to speak Danish . . . she said, 'Thank you for the blood' and with those words she passed into the presence of the Lord.

Questions to ponder and discuss

1. How has 'death lost its sting'?
2. What do you understand from Revelation 20 verses 14 and 15?
3. How can we comfort someone who has been bereaved?
4. Do you personally fear death?

Derek teaches us about death in *The End of Life's Journey*:

In the light of Christ's victory over death, I want to point you now to some promises that Jesus gave in anticipation of His victory. When He uses the phrase 'most assuredly', He introduces a statement that is absolutely authoritative.

> Most assuredly, I say to you, he who hears My word and believes in Him Who sent Me has everlasting life, and shall not come into judgement, but has passed from death into life.
> *John 5:24*

Notice that this is stated in the past tense. This is not something that is going to happen in the future. When we believe in the death and resurrection of Jesus Christ, by our faith, we have already passed from death into life. Death has no more dominion over us. Death has no more claims over us. Death is merely the gateway into a new life. In John 8:51-52 we have this assurance from Jesus Himself:

> Most assuredly, I say to you, if anyone keeps My word he shall never see death . . . If anyone keeps My word he shall never taste death.

Can you believe that? It is a promise from the lips of Jesus. He does not say that we will never experience physical death, but He says that those two evil angels, Death and Hades who follow behind him, have no more claims on us. They are excluded by the name and the blood of Jesus. So when death becomes our portion, we are going up into the very presence of God. This is guaranteed for us by the death and resurrection of Jesus on our behalf.

That is how it was with Stephen as he was facing martyrdom:

'Look!' (he cried) 'I see the heavens opened and the Son of Man standing at the right hand of God!' (And then a little further on, as he was being stoned, he said:) 'Lord Jesus, receive my spirit'. Then he knelt down and cried out with a loud voice, 'Lord, do not charge them with this sin.' And when he had said this, he fell asleep.
Acts 7:56, 59-60

We need to bear in mind that Scripture is very careful about the words it uses. As a rule it does not speak about believers dying. It speaks about them 'falling asleep.' For them death is only a temporary sleep out of which they will be awakened on the resurrection morning.

The Bible tells us:

Most assuredly, I say to you, he who hears My word and believes in Him who sent Me has everlasting life, and shall not come into judgement, but has passed from death into life.
John 5:24

But I do not want you to be ignorant, brethren, concerning those who have fallen asleep, lest you sorrow as others who have no hope. For if we believe that Jesus died and rose again, even so God will bring with Him those who sleep in Jesus (that is, those who have died in the faith.) For this we say to you by the word of the Lord, that we who are alive and remain until the coming of the Lord will by no means precede those who are asleep. For the Lord Himself will descend from heaven with a shout, with the voice of an archangel, and with the trumpet of God. And the dead in Christ will rise first. Then we who are alive and remain shall be caught up together with them in the clouds to meet the Lord in the air. And thus we

shall always be with the Lord. Therefore comfort one another with these words.
1 Thessalonians 4:13-18

So we are always confident, knowing that while we are at home in the body we are absent from the Lord . . . We are confident, yes, well pleased rather to be absent from the body and to be present with the Lord
2 Corinthians 5:6, 8

And many of those who sleep in the dust of the earth shall awake,
Some to everlasting life,
Some to shame and everlasting contempt.
Those who are wise shall shine
Like the brightness of the firmament,
And those who turn many to righteousness
Like the stars forever and ever.
Daniel 12:2-3

Marriage

Derek described how God had told him in a vision that the woman he had prayed for previously, was the woman God wanted him to marry. That woman was Ruth Baker.

In the early hours of the morning, a strange but vivid picture appeared before my eyes. I saw a hill sloping steeply towards me, a hill that reminded me of the one sloping up to Mount Zion at the southwest corner of the old City of Jerusalem. A zig-zag path wound its way up the hill from its base to its summit.

Instinctively I knew that this represented the path back to Jerusalem for me. It would climb steeply uphill all the way. There would be many sharp turns in it, first one way and then the other. But if I set my face and persevered, it would take me to the place God had appointed for me in Jerusalem.

The most striking feature in the picture I saw before me was the figure of a woman seated on the ground just at the point where the path started up the ill. Her features were European, her colouring blonde. But she was wearing what looked to be an Oriental-style dress, in a colour hard to define but predominantly green. What particularly struck me was her unusual posture. Her back was bent forward in a strained, unnatural position, suggesting pain. Suddenly I recognised her. It was Ruth Baker.

Questions to ponder and discuss

1. What is God's purpose for marriage?
2. Derek's experience of marriage was quite unique in that he allowed God to choose his partners for him. What is your opinion on this?
3. How can we help young people prepare for marriage?
4. What has God shown you about marriage?

Derek also tells us about marriage in *God is a Matchmaker*:

In each case, God worked according to His own plan for marriage, established at the dawn of human history. As it was with Lydia, so it has been with Ruth. God foresaw just the kind of wife I would need; He prepared her carefully for me; He placed her in the path He led me along; and He pointed her out to me as the helper that He had chosen for me.

In each case, too, the outworking of God's plan produced the union of two persons into one, which is His end purpose in marriage.

Derek also teaches about love in *Who Cares for Orphans, Widows, the Poor and Oppressed*:

Let me say this to you: the key to happiness is not being loved, it is having someone to love. That's what makes life exciting.

. . . I am suggesting that some of you need to break loose from your little religious mould and do something daring. After all, I did it. How many people would marry a woman and get eight daughters at the same time? And I tell you it was the making of me. It got me out of the religious rut. It got me involved with real people with real problems.

The Bible tells us:

It is not good for the man to be alone.
I will make a helper suitable for him.
Genesis 2:18

Then the Lord God made a woman from the rib he had taken out of the man, and he brought her to the man.
Genesis 2:22

Do not be yoked together with unbelievers.
For what do righteousness and wickedness
have in common?
Or what fellowship can have light with darkness?
What harmony is there between Christ and Belial?
What does a believer have in common with an unbeliever?
2 Corinthians 6:14-15 NIV

Who can find a virtuous wife?
For her worth is far above rubies.
The heart of her husband safely trusts her;
So he will have no lack of gain.
She does him good and not evil
All the days of her life.
Proverbs 31:10-12

'But from the beginning of the creation, God made them male and female.'

'For this reason a man shall leave his father and mother and be joined to his wife, and the two shall become one flesh'; so then they are no longer two, but one flesh.
Mark 10:6-8

Part Nine

Home to Jerusalem

Jerusalem

Derek tells us of his long association with Jerusalem and his special relationship with the Jews. He recalls how he once told a lady that he would like to live in Jerusalem. Derek tells us:

Her wise and prophetic answer was, 'You don't choose Jerusalem. Jerusalem chooses you!'

Questions to ponder and discuss

1. Why do you think there is so much emotion attached to discussions about Israel? (See page 57 and 58.)
2. What do you believe our response should be to the situation of the Jews?
3. Do you think we owe a debt to the Jews? (See page 56.)
4. Search out the Scriptures yourself to find out what God is saying to you.

Derek teaches us how to pray for Jerusalem in *Appointment in Jerusalem*. This is the story of his first wife - Lydia - as told to Derek:

Derek's first wife, Lydia, was led to Jerusalem by the Holy Spirit in 1928. She went through many trials and tribulations rescuing a Jewish child who would have died without her help and setting up a small children's home before Derek joined her in the work. When her mother wrote to her to see what help she needed, this is what she replied:

You ask what you can do to help. I believe there are some things that you – and every Christian – can do. In the midst of all the fighting God showed me something which has changed my whole outlook.

I suddenly came to see that we Christians have a debt that has gone unpaid for many centuries – to Israel and to Jerusalem. It is to them that we owe the Bible, the prophets, the apostles, the Saviour Himself. For far too long we have forgotten this debt, but now the time has come for us to begin repaying it – and there are two ways that we can do this.

First, we need to repent of our sins against Israel: at best, our lack of gratitude and concern; at worse, our open contempt and persecution.

Then, out of true love and concern, we must pray as the psalmist tells us, 'for the peace of Jerusalem', remembering that peace can only come to Jerusalem as Israel turns back to God. God has shown me that from now on to pray in this way for Jerusalem will be the highest form of service that I can render Him.

Derek teaches us about Israel in *The Destiny of Israel and the Church*:

Why is Israel the focus of attention in the world's media? Why do leaders of governments, who are normally pragmatic and statesmanlike, erupt with emotional outbursts when Israel is discussed? Why does the United Nations devote thirty per cent of its time and one third of its resolutions to Israel – a tiny country with a population of only five million?

There is only one source for a clear and authoritative answer: the Bible. Although it was completed millennia before the current problems in the Middle East arose, the Bible provides a supernaturally inspired analysis of both the issues and the forces that are involved.

Israel occupies a unique place in the current controversies because the place which Israel occupies in God's purposes is likewise unique. The prophetic word of God reveals that this present age will culminate with the restoration and redemption of Israel. The nearer we come to the close of the age, therefore, the more intense will be the pressures surrounding Israel.

These events that centre around Israel will also determine the destiny of Satan, the age-old adversary of God and man. In 2 Corinthians 4:4 Satan is called 'the god of this age'. He is well aware that when Israel's redemption is completed and this age closes, he will no longer be able to pose as a god. He will be stripped of his power to deceive and manipulate humanity, and he will be subject to the judgement of God. Consequently, he is at this time deploying all his deceptive strategy and exercising all his evil power to resist the process of Israel's restoration.

Here then are the two main spiritual forces that meet in conflict over the Middle East: on the one hand, the grace of God working toward Israel's restoration; and on the other hand, the deceitful strategies of Satan, opposing by every means in his power the process of restoration. This is the real, but invisible reason, for the struggles and tensions to which Israel is currently being subjected.

Derek teaches us from the Scriptures that God has warned the nations that 'there is a time coming when He will call the nations to account for their high-handed actions in regard to the land of Israel.'

> I will also gather all nations,
> And bring them down to the Valley of Jehoshaphat;
> And I will enter into judgement with them there
> On account of My people, My heritage Israel,
> Whom they have scattered among the nations;
> They have also divided up My land.
> *Joel 3:2*

God says that a remnant will be saved.

> And it shall come to pass in all the land,
> Says the Lord,
> That two thirds in it shall be cut off and die.
> But one third shall be left in it.
> I will bring one third through the fire,
> Will refine them as silver is refined,
> And test them as gold is tested.
> They will call on my name,
> And I will answer them.
> I will say, 'This is My people,'
> And each one will say,
> 'The Lord is my God.'
> *Zechariah 13:8-9*

> God said to Israel through the prophet Jeremiah:
> I have loved you with an everlasting love
> *Jeremiah 31:3*

The Bible also tells us:

The Lord God . . . swore to me (Abraham), saying, 'To your descendants I give this land.'
Genesis 24:7

'. . . to you (Isaac) and your descendants I give all these lands, and I will perform the oath which I swore to Abraham your father.'
Genesis 26:3

And Joseph said to his brethren, . . . 'God will . . . bring you out of this land to the land of which He swore to Abraham, to Isaac, and to Jacob.'
Genesis 50:24

'And I will bring you (Israel) into the land which I swore to give to Abraham, Isaac, and Jacob; and I will give it to you as a heritage: I am the Lord.'
Exodus 6:8

'And it shall be, when the Lord brings you into the land of the Canaanites and the Hittites and the Amorites and the Hivites and the Jebusites, which He swore to your fathers to give you . . .'
Exodus 13:5

He (the Lord) remembers His covenant for ever,
The word which He commanded, for a thousand generations,
The covenant which he made with Abraham,
And His oath to Isaac,
And confirmed it to Jacob for a statute,
To Israel as an everlasting covenant,
Saying, 'To you I will give the land of Canaan . . .'
Psalm 105:8-11

'Then I (the Lord) brought them into the land concerning which I had raised My hand in an oath to give them . . .'
Ezekiel 20:28

Looking Back on a Long Life

Derek looks back over his life with complete honesty and tells us:

If I were to look back . . . I would say the mistakes I have made are more in motivation. I was an only child, without brothers or sisters and I was by nature a very self-centred person and God has only delivered me from self-centredness very gradually over time . . . I would wish I could have had a different attitude towards some of my fellow Christians. There is a little song which says, 'He looked beyond my thoughts and saw my needs', and that is where I have had to change and view my fellow Christians – looking beyond their faults and seeing their needs. In fact God has brought me to that place to an amazing extent because when I talk to people now and their needs are exposed, I begin to feel their need is my need. So God has been very gracious to me and I give Him all the glory, but what He has really been dealing with, is my own character and my priorities; they have changed significantly over the years.

Questions to ponder and discuss

1 Do you agree with Derek's comment 'How quickly and easily, as God's servants, we tend to forget that every success in our ministry should prompt us to self-humbling in response to God's unmerited favour!'? (See page 61.) Discuss.

2 How do you think this video of Derek's life has affected you?

3. Which part has had the most impact?

Derek writes in *War in Heaven*:

I look back now over more than sixty years in Christian service and I am shocked to realise that men and women called and equipped by God are still today making the same tragic error that Lucifer made. I am reminded continually of a Chinese pastor who spent more than twenty years in prison for his faith. He said, 'I've seen many Christians have a good beginning, but few have a good ending.' How quickly and easily, as God's servants, we tend to forget that every success in our ministry should prompt us to self-humbling in response to God's unmerited favour!

Derek points us to Jesus as the pattern of humility.

Paul vividly depicts the self-humbling of Jesus in Philippians 2:

> Who, being in the form of God, did not consider it robbery to be equal with God, but made Himself of no reputation, taking the form of a bondservant, and coming in the likeness of men. And being found in appearance as a man, He humbled Himself and become obedient to the point of death, even the death of the cross.
> *Verses 6-8*

These verses outline for us seven great downward steps that Jesus took from heaven's glory to His death on the cross:

- *'He made Himself of no reputation'. Literally, He emptied Himself. As Charles Wesley says in one of his hymns, 'Christ emptied Himself of all but love.'*
- *'He took upon Himself the form of a servant.' He was the 'LORD of glory,' but He stepped down to become a servant.*

- *'He was made in the likeness of men.' He became a member of the Adamic race, made a little lower than the angels.*
- *'He was found in fashion (appearance) as a man.' He looked just like a normal man of His own day. There was nothing external to distinguish Him from the people He lived among.*
- *'He humbled Himself.' He was a humble man. He was not a priest or a ruler, but a carpenter's son.*
- *'He became obedient unto death.' His perfect obedience brought Him ultimately to His atoning death for sinful humanity.*
- *'He became obedient to the death of a criminal on the Cross.' Crucifixion was the agonizing penalty for the worst person who had committed the most heinous crime.*

These are the seven great downward steps that the Lord Jesus took. But the seven great downward steps led to the seven great upward steps that are described in verses 9-11.

> Therefore God also has highly exalted Him and given Him the name which is above every name, that at the name of Jesus every knee should bow, of those in heaven, and of those on earth, and of those under the earth, and that every tongue should confess that Jesus Christ is Lord, to the glory of God the Father.

Here we have the seven upward steps of the exaltation of Jesus:
- *'God has highly exalted Him.'*
- *'God has given Him a name that is above every name.'*
- *'At the name of Jesus, every knee shall bow.'*
- *'Of those in heaven' – that is, all the created hosts who serve God in His heaven.*
- *'Of those on earth.' This means that ultimately every creature on earth will submit to the authority of Christ.*
- *'Of those under the earth.' This refers to Satan's realm in Hades. It includes death, hell, the grave and also the unrighteous dead who had previously rejected God's mercy.*
- *'Every tongue shall confess that Jesus Christ is Lord.' The Lordship of Jesus will be proclaimed in every area of the universe.*

The Bible also tells us:

Humility and the fear of the Lord bring wealth and honour and life.
Proverbs 22:4 NIV

The fear of the Lord is to hate evil;
Pride and arrogance and the evil way
And the perverse mouth I hate.
Proverbs 8:13

Before destruction the heart of a man is haughty.
And before honour is humility.
Proverbs 18:12

If My people who are called by My name will humble themselves, and pray and seek My face, and turn from their wicked ways, then I will hear from heaven, and will forgive their sin and heal their land.
2 Chronicles 7:14